The Only Way is Ethics

As Long as You Love Me

Divorce and remarriage

Sean Doherty

21 20 19 18 17 16 15   7 6 5 4 3 2 1

First published 2015 by Authentic Media Limited,
52 Presley Way, Crownhill, Milton Keynes, MK8 0ES.
authenticmedia.co.uk

British Library Cataloguing in Publication Data
A catalogue record for this book is available from the British Library.
ISBN: 978-1-78078-149-5
978-1-78078-438-0 (e-book)

Cover design by Sara Garcia

Marriage is popular. In England and Wales, there are about a quarter of a million weddings a year. But only a tiny proportion of people are virgins when they marry, and 85 per cent of couples are already living together when they tie the knot. It's estimated that 42 per cent of all marriages in England and Wales end in divorce.[1] Divorce doesn't necessarily put people off – in more than a third of marriages today, one or both partners have been married previously.[2] So the popularity of marriage doesn't necessarily mean that people are signing up to the Christian ideal (and here as in my other writing in this series I'm assuming marriage as being between a woman and a man).

An older way of seeing marriage was as a way of life or institution. You were free not to join it, but if you did join, you didn't get to set the terms. Now, it's more of a contract. The terms you set should be demanding, because the consumer deserves the best. And if those terms are not met, if your service provider does not live up to your legitimate expectations, then they have broken the contract, and you may walk away. Marriage is conditional on a good performance.

---

[1] See http://www.ons.gov.uk/ons/rel/vsob1/divorces-in-england-and-wales/2011/sty-what-percentage-of-marriages-end-in-divorce.html. Throughout what follows, I use the most recently available data which is for England and Wales in 2012.

[2] See http://www.ons.gov.uk/ons/rel/vsob1/marriages-in-england-and-wales--provisional-/2012/index.html.

A big influence today is romanticism – the idea that we should be in a relationship with the person that is 'right' for us. (Before marriage of course couples should discern carefully whether they are suited.) The problem comes when romanticism breaks up existing relationships – when one spouse decides someone else is really the right one for them. Rather than being true to their spouse and the bond they already have, they must be true to themselves. New and more powerful feelings of love and romance are more decisive than prior commitments.

The reality is that in marriage you quickly discover that Mr or Mrs Right is not perfect, and neither are you! In any case, sharing your life with another person, in addition to the normal pressures and changes of life, changes you both. A marriage that is conditional on somebody staying the same cannot last: only God is wonderful enough to stay eternally interesting without ever changing. Rather, marriage needs to be secure enough that you can change and grow safely. For this to happen, we have to replace the romantic ideal with something more domestic and less glamorous but ultimately more glorious and transformative.[3]

In what follows, I'll look at the legal realities of divorce in the UK today, the reasons why in the Bible God is generally so opposed to divorce, and whether there are circumstances in which it is right to seek divorce or to get

---

[3]See Timothy Keller with Kathy Keller, *The Meaning of Marriage: Facing the Complexities of Marriage with the Wisdom of God* (London: Hodder & Stoughton, 2011), ch. 1.

remarried. I will also offer some suggestions and further resources for those who want to support women who experience domestic abuse.

Divorce today

In Britain today you can't just get divorced. You have to prove that the marriage has already irretrievably broken down on one of several grounds.[4] In 2012, 14 per cent of divorces were on the grounds that one party had committed adultery.[5]

The most common reason, which accounts for 48 per cent of divorces, is that one of the parties had persistently demonstrated 'unreasonable behaviour'. This is probably the most popular ground because it is the quickest route to divorce unless adultery has taken place. 'Unreasonable behaviour' could include physical violence, emotional abuse, addiction, financial irresponsibility, not showing interest in one's spouse, and (persistent) refusal to co-operate with household chores.

Provided the divorce is uncontested, in practice the courts grant divorces for more mild reasons. Let's face it,

---

[4]Divorce is different to annulment, which is the recognition that a marriage was never valid in the first place (for example, if one of the parties was not of sound mind at the time of the wedding). The Roman Catholic Church also grants religious annulments, which have no legal force.

[5]For this and the statistics that follow, see http://www.ons.gov.uk/ons/ rel/vsob1/divorces-in-england-and-wales/2012/stb-divorces-2012. html.

it's not hard to find examples of unreasonable behaviour in any marriage. As one divorce solicitor puts it:

> The courts adopt a realistic attitude. They know that if one party to a marriage . . . issue[s] a divorce petition the marriage has irretrievably broken down . . . and it would be futile to pretend otherwise. The courts therefore adopt quite a relaxed attitude.[6]

Some solicitors therefore advise the petitioner to make the allegations serious enough to warrant divorce, but not serious enough for the other spouse to contest them. The grounds for divorce do not normally prejudice financial settlements and custody of any children, removing a possible incentive for someone to dispute the allegations.

With adultery and unreasonable behaviour, one of the parties is at fault: they caused the marriage to break down. Divorce can also be granted when there is 'no fault', if the couple have been separated for two years and if the other party consents (which accounts for 26 per cent of divorces), or for five years even without consent (which accounts for 12 per cent).

So, the vast majority of divorces in the UK today are either 'no fault' divorces or 'unreasonable behaviour' divorces. Of course, we can't tell from the statistics which of the 56,500 divorces granted for 'unreasonable behaviour' involved cases of cruel or abusive behaviour, and which ones involved the courts being 'relaxed'.

---

[6]'Reasons for Divorce: Unreasonable Behaviour', online at http://www.terry.co.uk/unreasonable_behaviour.html.

It's now time to look at why divorce is so problematic from God's perspective, before we consider when the Bible allows it.

Why is God generally so opposed to divorce?

God values marriage very highly and is generally opposed to divorce. For example: 'The wife should not separate from her husband (but if she does, she should remain unmarried or else be reconciled to her husband), and the husband should not divorce his wife' (1 Cor. 7:10–11). Although Jesus and Paul make exceptions to this principle, it is clearly a strong one. To many people today this seems legalistic and unrealistic, so it's important to explore why the Bible is so opposed to divorce and remarriage in general – for theologically important and pastorally loving reasons.

1. Divorce rips apart two people that God has bound together as 'one flesh' (Gen. 2:24). This is the reason that Jesus himself gives as to why divorce should not take place: 'What therefore God has joined together, let not man separate' (Matt. 19:6). He does not say nobody *can* separate, but that nobody *should* do so.[7] Divorce is so painful and devastating because there cannot be a neat separation of two different people: they have become one. This is true whether the marriage is between Christians or not.

---

[7] This is why I find the Roman Catholic view that divorce is impossible unconvincing. For that teaching, see *Catechism of the Catholic Church*, Part 3, Section 2, Chapter 2, Article 6, online at http://www.vatican.va/archive/ccc_css/archive/catechism/p3s2c2a6.htm.

2. Human decree cannot simply undo what God has done. Some divorces may take place properly in the eyes of the law, but not in reality. This is why Jesus describes remarriage after divorce as adultery. That is, the previous marriage still exists, even if it has been dissolved legally.

3. Marriage is not just a convenient biological mechanism to make babies, nor simply a pragmatic way of protecting relationships. God gave the 'one flesh' union of wife and husband to reflect God's relationship of absolute love for and commitment to God's people. Marriage is a picture of how closely and intimately we are united to Jesus Christ, and of how God never gives up on us, no matter what we do. Divorce is possible, but it is always a tragedy, because it falls short of God's wonderful purpose for marriage: to be a picture of the gospel.

4. The Bible's restrictions on divorce protect the vulnerable, especially women and children. When the Bible was written, women had few rights and little power over their own lives. Divorce could usually only be initiated by men, and often left the woman with children to support and no easy prospect of earning a living. Today, in theory, women have better employment prospects, and we expect fathers to contribute financially to their children's care. But unequal pay is still widespread, and more than 90 per cent of lone parents are women. Overall, women still bear the financial and practical brunt of marital breakdown.

5. By working through the challenges that all marriages face, couples come face to face with their sinfulness and selfishness, and have the opportunity to repent

and find greater freedom from sin. Divorce can be an escape from this hard but necessary path of transformation. (This point should not be misused to encourage anyone to stay with someone who is abusing them. Abuse is not the same as run-of-the-mill selfishness.)

So, divorce is mostly forbidden and criticised in the Bible because it is usually an exploitative practice that favours men, places an unfair burden on women, causes great personal pain, harms children, fails to bear witness to the gospel significance of marriage, and avoids the liberating but costly self-sacrifice that makes us more like Christ. Yet even so, there are times when the Bible permits divorce and remarriage, and we will look at these now.

The Old Testament attitude to divorce

The Old Testament is ambivalent about divorce. For example, Deuteronomy 24:1–4 acknowledges that divorce takes place. But it does not encourage divorce so much as limit the damage after divorce by saying that a divorced woman should not go back to her first husband if she is unlucky enough to get divorced again.

Another key passage is Exodus 21:10–11. It says that if a man has taken a slave as a wife and then wants another wife as well, he may not 'diminish [the first wife's] food, her clothing, or her marital rights [i.e. affection and sex]' (v. 10). If he neglects her in these ways, he must free her without her having to pay money to redeem herself from slavery (v. 11).

But is this passage really about divorce? The point of the law is to protect women who have already been enslaved and married regardless of their wishes from the consequences of polygamy. The outcome for such women is not divorce as such, but freedom from slavery. Again, the purpose was damage limitation.

So, the Old Testament recognises that divorce, slavery and polygamy happen, but that doesn't mean it approves of them. Rather, the Law mitigates them and protects their victims. It's a bit like the Slave Trade Act of 1807. This outlawed the slave trade, but it did not set existing slaves free. That came later. At the time, outlawing the trade was the best that the abolitionists could get, and it was better than nothing. You could even say that in a sense the Act of 1807 continued to allow slavery. But that doesn't mean it was in favour of it. It was just that the Act needed enough political support to pass. Law, like politics, is the art of the possible.

Similarly, the Old Testament divorce laws are damage limitation. If divorce was simply illegal, vulnerable women would be worse off. Some husbands would still abandon their wives, who would remain legally married and therefore unable to marry again. In some societies in the ancient world, the husband could come back and reclaim his wife and children later if it suited him, so other men would be reluctant to marry a divorcee.[8] The Law therefore limits divorce to certain circumstances, so that husbands could

---

[8]See David Instone-Brewer, *Divorce and Remarriage in the Church: Biblical Solutions for Pastoral Realities* (Milton Keynes: Paternoster, 2011), Kindle edition, ch. 2.

not abandon women on a whim or because they wanted a new wife, and the Law requires a husband to give his wife a certificate of divorce so that her freedom to remarry was publicly recognised. In this sense, the Law allows divorce. But that doesn't mean it approves. The intention was to protect the people who had the most to lose. The Law allows divorce, precisely in order to regulate it.

Reasons for divorce in the Old Testament

So, when *does* the Law allow divorce? Exodus 21:11, as we have seen, requires a husband to set his slave wife free without payment if he diminished her 'food, her clothing, or her marital rights'. Some therefore conclude that God allowed divorce if someone deprives their spouse in any of these ways. But remember that the woman in this case is a slave, so the solution to her plight is freedom, not divorce. Also, the point of the law was to protect the first wife in a polygamous marriage from being deprived rather than to set out a general rule for divorce in monogamous marriages. The principle here is that polygamous men must treat all their wives properly, not that divorce may take place when any husband deprives his wife of food, clothing or love.

Going back to Deuteronomy 24:1, divorce was legitimate if the husband 'found some indecency' in his wife. The Hebrew for 'indecency' is *erwat dabar*, which literally means 'a matter (or cause) of nakedness'. This refers to sexual immorality such as adultery or if the wife turns out not to have been a virgin when she got married. If we take it literally, it could even mean a woman being naked in public. So, since I have argued that Exodus 21:11 does not refer to divorce in general, the only time that the Law actually allowed divorce was when a woman had been sexually immoral.[9]

Does God say 'I hate divorce'?

One frequently quoted verse about divorce is Malachi 2:16, which some Bible versions translate as 'I hate divorce.' If they are right, this seems like a 'clobber text', ruling out divorce in general. But this reads more into the text than it says. Whilst it is hardly a ringing endorsement of divorce, it does not say, 'divorce is impossible', or 'divorce should never take place'. The phrase simply expresses God's general feelings about it.

More importantly, the 'clobber' approach rips the verse out of its context. The passage in which it occurs (Mal. 2:13–16) refers to the practice of a man divorcing 'the

----

[9]It is only fair to let readers know that my interpretation differs from a leading authority on this subject, David Instone-Brewer (see his *Divorce and Remarriage in the Church*, ch. 3). He argues that divorce is legitimate for four reasons: failure to provide food, or clothing, lack of conjugal love (including but not only sex), and sexual infidelity. Abuse would also be a legitimate reason for divorce, since it is an extreme version of lack of love. Instone-Brewer suggests that these four grounds for divorce reflect the four marriage vows: to provide food, to provide clothing, to love and to be faithful. He therefore concludes that the Law allows divorce if someone breaks their marriage vows. But the texts themselves make no reference to the marriage vows being broken. And there are very few marriages where there has never been a withdrawal of marital love. Instone-Brewer doesn't want the slippery slope this introduces – but it is not clear to me that he can protect against it.

in such a profound way that the victim may divorce them and remarry.

Divorce in such circumstances is not compulsory. God delights in bringing about repentance and reconciliation. Leaping into divorce too quickly might forego an opportunity for God-given restoration. But other times the trust and bond of marriage are damaged irrevocably, hence the victim of adultery is not sinning by initiating a divorce.

So why is there a difference between Mark and Matthew? Mark wrote before Matthew, and Matthew used Mark as a basis for his own gospel. So, if Matthew used Mark's account of Jesus's teaching on divorce, why did he add the words 'except *porneia*', where previously no exceptions were allowed to the prohibition of divorce? One explanation is that Matthew is toning down Mark's supposedly overly strict teaching. I don't find this convincing, because Matthew is first in the queue when it comes to pointing out when the standards of the Law are too weak.

The answer to the conundrum is in the question the Pharisees ask Jesus in Matthew 19:3: 'Is it lawful to divorce one's wife *for any cause*?' Matthew has also added the phrase 'for any cause' (see Mark 10:2). This reflects a heated debate between two then-prominent rabbis, Hillel and Shammai.

Shammai tended to be stricter than Hillel. For example, Hillel permitted white lies and Shammai did not. When it came to Deuteronomy 24:1, which permitted divorce if someone found 'indecency' in his wife, Shammai thought that 'indecency' meant only sexual indecency, especially adultery, whilst Hillel argued that 'indecency' meant anything displeasing about her, including spoiling the dinner. In other words, Hillel permitted divorce 'for any cause'. Both agreed that divorce could take place if either party withdrew food, clothing, or conjugal love (because of Exod. 21:10–11).

So, when the Pharisees in Mark 10:2 asked Jesus whether divorce was lawful, they were not asking him a general question. They were asking him *where he stood in this debate*. They had no need to say 'for any cause', because everyone agreed that divorce was lawful. The question was whether it was lawful for any reason or not. And when Jesus said it was not lawful, he had no need to add 'except for adultery', because everyone knew that was lawful. If someone asks, 'Do you drink?' we know they mean, 'Do you drink alcohol?' Or, if a man asks his wife, 'Shall I wear a jacket over this shirt?' and she replies, 'Just wear the shirt,' she would be shocked if he did not put on any trousers![13]

Mark simply records the words more or less as they were spoken. Everyone knew that divorce for sexual immorality was acceptable, so he doesn't need to spell this out. But Matthew, writing later on, adds 'for any cause' and 'except for sexual immorality' to clarify what Jesus originally meant, namely that you can't get divorced 'for any cause', but only for *porneia*.

---

[13] These examples are adapted from David Instone-Brewer, *Divorce and Remarriage in the Church*, ch. 5.

Jesus was often counter-cultural. Here he is being even stricter than the already-strict Shammai.[14] Jesus allows divorce after sexual immorality, but he does not mention withdrawal of food, clothing or love (not surprising given that Exod. 21 isn't really about divorce). His words in Matthew 5:31–32 corroborate this. There, Jesus is not responding to a question about Hillelite 'any cause' divorce, so his words cannot refer to that. Instead, it is a *general* prohibition of divorce, the only exception to which is *porneia*. Clearly, Jesus is normally opposed to divorce, with the exception of when sexual immorality (primarily adultery) has taken place. Adultery violates the 'one flesh' nature of marriage so deeply that divorce does not initiate marital break-up so much as recognize that break-up has already happened.

Legitimate divorce 2: being unwillingly divorced

Earlier, I quoted 1 Corinthians 7:10–11, where Paul states his general view (based on Jesus's teaching), that married couples should not 'separate'. If they have, they should either seek reconciliation or, if this is not possible, remain unmarried.

The reason Paul uses the word 'separate' is that, in the Greco-Roman context of Corinth, divorce happened simply

---

[14]This is evident in the fact that Jesus astonishes his disciples by what he says, so that they almost renounce marriage: 'If such is the case of a man with his wife, it is better not to marry' (Matt. 19:10). It's unlikely that they would be so surprised if Jesus was just advocating one of the standard views of the day.

by the couple separating. This is evident in what Paul says next: 'If any brother has a wife who is an unbeliever, and she consents to live with him, he should not divorce her. If any woman has a husband who is an unbeliever, and he consents to live with her, she should not divorce him' (vv. 12–13). What is decisive is 'living with', because divorce happened through separation. In other words, divorce was extremely easy.

Whilst Christians shouldn't initiate divorce, Paul adds that 'if the unbelieving partner separates, let it be so' (v. 15). A Christian should not initiate a separation just because they are married to a non-Christian. But if the non-Christian leaves, let them, so that you can live 'at peace' with others. You don't need to try to make them stay. When a non-Christian divorces a Christian, the Christian is 'not enslaved' (v. 15). (The next section explains why this means that they are free to remarry.)

But what if a Christian is divorced by another Christian? I think they are also free to remarry. For Paul, the fact that one spouse is a Christian and one is not does not soften the marriage bond. What destroys the bond in Paul's example must be the divorce itself.

So, whilst nobody should initiate divorce unless adultery has taken place, people who have been divorced against their will have done nothing wrong and are free to remarry. Similarly, they are not obliged to oppose a divorce petition (although, of course, they may have good reasons for doing so) because Paul says, 'Let it be so . . . God has called you to peace' (v. 15). This is important today because it could mean the difference between having to wait two years after separation rather than five.

When can a divorcee get remarried?

So, we have seen that Jesus allowed people to initiate divorce for adultery, and Paul says that someone who has been divorced by their spouse is 'not enslaved' (1 Cor. 7:15). Does this mean that the victims of divorce and adultery may remarry, or simply that they are not obliged to try to maintain their previous marriage?

One view is that, because Jesus describes remarriage after divorce as adultery, real divorce is never possible: marriage is indissoluble. The original couple is still one flesh, even if they are living separately and indeed even if they have remarried. When Jesus permitted divorce after adultery, he meant only separation 'from bed and board', in Augustine's phrase. This view can also appeal to 1 Corinthians 7:11: 'she should remain unmarried or else be reconciled to her husband'.

I do not find this view persuasive, as 1 Corinthians 7:11 is addressed to people who have initiated divorce, not to its victims. And, as we have seen, Matthew 19:9 describes remarriage after divorce as adultery *except* when it follows sexual immorality. The implication is that remarriage after sexual immorality is not adultery, which must mean that the original marriage has truly ended. But most importantly, in Jesus's context, divorce meant by definition that you could marry again. The Jewish divorce certificate said simply, 'You are free to marry any [Jewish] man you wish.'[15] By permitting divorce after adultery, Jesus permitted remarriage too.

Similarly, the phrase, 'not enslaved' in 1 Corinthians 7:15 must mean, 'free to remarry'. Under Roman law, you obtained the freedom to remarry simply by separating from your previous spouse. This is corroborated by the fact that Paul uses the same word in verses 27 and 39 to say wife and husband are 'bound' together, which he contrasts with being 'free' to marry (see also Rom. 7:2–3). Not being bound means being able to marry. So, Paul permits a victim of divorce to remarry, but not the initiator of the divorce (1Cor. 7–11) (although I find Instone-Brewer's argument convincing that even the latter could remarry if their original spouse does, i.e. once reconciliation is no longer possible).[16]

Is there a contradiction between the teachings of Jesus and Paul?

It might look like it. Jesus says that we should never initiate divorce, except after adultery. But Paul allows remarriage if a non-Christian leaves a Christian. Isn't this a second reason for divorce?

I don't think this is a contradiction, for the simple reason that Jesus speaks of when someone can rightly *initiate* divorce, whereas Paul is saying that you can remarry when someone has *already divorced you*.

---

[15]*Divorce and Remarriage in the Church*, ch. 2.
[16]*Divorce and Remarriage in the Church*, ch. 9.

Violence and abuse[17]

I have argued that, according to Jesus, someone can only legitimately initiate divorce when their spouse has committed adultery, that nobody is obliged to resist divorce, and that someone who has been divorced or has initiated divorce following adultery is free to remarry.

But there are other situations when it is difficult or dangerous for a couple to remain together. The most obvious example is abuse. Abuse takes many forms. Physical abuse may include pushing someone, pulling their hair, preventing them from taking medication, restricting their freedom, damaging their property or exhausting them. Emotional abuse may include humiliating someone, preventing someone from maintaining good relationships with friends and family, name-calling, constant criticism, and making threats. It may be sexual, such as forcing someone to do sexual acts, rejecting them sexually, or interfering with contraception. It can be financial: preventing someone from working (or forcing them to work), controlling the finances, or expecting someone to account for every penny.

Research estimates that one in four women suffer abuse from a partner. Two women a week are killed by their partners or former partners, and more die by suicide to escape abuse.[18] Of course, men can also experience abuse. And there are other behaviours that are extremely hurtful and difficult to live with too, such as

---

[17]I am very grateful to Natalie Collins of Spark for her generous help with this section. See http://www.sparkequip.org/.

[18]See http://www.refuge.org.uk/.

financial irresponsibility, addiction, and someone ceasing to show any interest in or love towards a spouse. In such cases, it seems unfair to us today, and in some circumstances very dangerous, that anyone should remain trapped in such marriages.

Someone who is being hurt and/or controlled by their partner should not hesitate to get appropriate outside support, including the police where relevant (including co-operating with any investigation and prosecution).[19] Some Christians may hold back from involving the police, because of Jesus's teaching that they should turn the other cheek. Of course, they are correct not to respond violently, although they may need to act in self-defence or to defend their children.[20] But domestic violence is not a private matter. It is a crime. We must read 'turn the other cheek' alongside passages such as Romans 13, which says that God has established the governing authorities to deter and punish wrongdoing. The Bible speaks frequently of God's care for the vulnerable and victimised, which is precisely why God gives civil government. The weak should therefore certainly seek help from the (admittedly imperfect) institutions that God has made to

---

[19]The 24 Hour National Domestic Violence Helpline on 0808 2000 247 provides information about such support, and see www.womensaid. org.uk and http://www.refuge.org.uk/. See also Restored, a Christian alliance seeking to end violence against women: http://www.restore-drelationships.org/.

[20]Where children are involved, church members and leaders must obviously follow proper safeguarding policies, which will invariably include reporting concerns to the proper authorities.

protect them. It is important to remember this because, usually, abusive spouses are highly manipulative and act in a sorrowful way to try to persuade their victim to stay with them.

If the perpetrator is not removed or willing to leave whilst they get professional help, the person experiencing abuse should not hesitate to leave the marital home (and take any children with them). This is for their safety but, in a sense, this is also helping the abusive partner by hopefully depriving him (or her) of further opportunities to commit very serious sins. If a woman experiencing abuse chooses to leave, she is very likely to need support and help to do so, because trying to leave can actually make things more dangerous for her.

The person who is being hurt may feel obliged to stick by their spouse and be faithful to their marriage. But as well as teaching against divorce and remarriage, Jesus also teaches on dealing openly with sin:

> If your brother sins against you, go and tell him his fault, between you and him alone. If he listens to you, you have gained your brother. But if he does not listen, take one or two others along with you, that every charge may be established by the evidence of two or three witnesses. If he refuses to listen to them, tell it to the church. And if he refuses to listen even to the church, let him be to you as a Gentile and a tax collector.
>
> *Matthew 18:15–17*

So turning the other cheek does not mean ignoring wrongdoing or allowing people to mistreat you. It means handling wrongdoing the right way, which may well include involving others. For Jesus, confrontation needs community. So, someone who is experiencing abuse need not feel guilty or disloyal about involving other people by getting help. Whatever else has happened, abuse is always the responsibility of the perpetrator and never the fault of the victim.

Church members and leaders must listen to and take seriously any claim of abuse, and must involve specialist domestic abuse services immediately.[21] Whatever someone has disclosed is likely to be the tip of the iceberg, and many perpetrators will try to co-opt church leaders and members as allies. The purpose of abuse is to gain power and control over someone, and so our role involves empowering the person who has been hurt. Too often the church has colluded with or covered up abuse, whereas Jesus teaches that those who refuse to repent of their sin must be exposed. (Not that church leaders should confront the abuser themselves, as this is likely to put the person suffering abuse at risk.)

Expressions of sorrow and promises not to do it again are not enough. Repentance is not simply remorse. It includes taking concrete steps to put it right, such as leaving the marital home whilst they engage fully with any criminal processes and get proper help to change their

---

[21]See footnote 20 for details. Also see *Ending Domestic Abuse*, a useful pack for churches produced by Restored, online at: http://www.restoredrelationships.org/resources/info/51/.

behaviour.[22] If they are not willing to take such steps, they are not really acknowledging the seriousness of their crime and sin. That is, they are not yet repentant. A good biblical example here is Joseph in Genesis 44. Rather than seeking reconciliation immediately, Joseph first tests his brothers to see if they have changed. His goal is still reconciliation, but reconciliation (unlike forgiveness) requires true repentance on the part of the wrongdoer.

If there is no repentance and restitution, ultimately the Christian fellowship must exclude the perpetrator. In other words, there is a genuine basis in Jesus's teaching for a victim to separate from the perpetrator. The purpose of discipline is not to punish someone, but to show them the serious consequences of their unwillingness to repent. The hope is that showing them what God must eventually do to them if they do not repent will bring them to repentance (1 Cor. 5:5). Separation here is not judgement or punishment, but love.

But is someone obliged to remain married to someone who has abused them, or could abuse be a legitimate reason for divorce? The best way to argue for this would be by analogy with adultery. Jesus allowed divorce and remarriage following adultery, because adultery is such a

---

[22]That is, accessing an accredited perpetrator programme. Counselling, anger management, addiction treatment, pastoral care and/or marriage courses are all helpful in other circumstances, but are not adequate programmes for perpetrators of domestic abuse. For information on such programmes, call Respect on 0808 802 4040 or see http://www.respectphoneline.org.uk/pages/domestic-violence-prevention-programmes.html.

profound violation of marriage that it effectively renders the marriage over (unless the victim chooses to forgive). So you could argue that Jesus would also allow divorce for abuse, which is an equivalent kind of violation to adultery.

However, although I have said that it is essential to leave a dangerous situation, to seek professional help, and to separate permanently if the perpetrator of abuse does not repent, I have to say that I cannot see a biblical basis for initiating divorce in such circumstances. Jesus only gave one exception to his prohibition of divorce and I don't think we can add to that. I am very aware that this conclusion will seem very unfair to some, and of course other theologians have reached different conclusions.[23] All I would ask is that if you do reach a different point of view, you do so on the basis of the Bible.

If someone wrongly initiated a divorce, should they try to return to their first marriage?

If neither party has remarried and both are willing, reconciliation can be wonderful – although some good relationship counselling and support will almost certainly be needed. If you initiated a divorce that you now believe was wrong, but your ex-spouse is not willing to try reconciliation, I think you should probably stay single, unless they remarry. But if either or both of you have remarried, then your previous marriage certainly has ended, even if the original marriage was not broken by the legal divorce. If so, whilst you repent

----

[23]For example, see Barbara Roberts, *Not Under Bondage: Biblical Divorce for Abuse, Adultery and Desertion* (Australia: Maschil Press, 2008), ch. 3.

of what you have done and seek to put it right in other ways, don't break up your new marriage in order to return to an original one. Two wrongs don't make a right!

Should divorcees remarry in church?

Churches have to make some very tough calls when approached by couples who wish to remarry in church. Many will be faithful church members, whom the church already cares for personally. Others may not be Christians at all, and the church will rightly want them to feel accepted and loved, so that they may discover Jesus for themselves.

Some churches and ministers refuse to conduct marriages if people are divorced and their ex-spouse is still living, because Jesus describes remarriage as being adultery in most circumstances. Even though divorce has legally taken place, the original couple is still married. This approach is rightly cautious of sanctioning adultery, but it ignores the fact that the Bible allows remarriage after divorce in some circumstances.

At the opposite extreme, other churches allow anyone to be remarried, because it is up to the couple to decide whether or not their marriage is right in the sight of God. This is somewhat naïve. Yes, we should show everyone God's grace. But forgiveness does not abolish the consequences of what we have done, and one consequence of getting married is that you cannot usually become unmarried. A minister who prevents a couple from entering into what Jesus describes as an adulterous relationship is being kind and not judgemental.

The advantage of both these extremes is that the church (or minister) does not act as judge and jury over individual cases. Churches are neither resourced nor trained to investigate and apportion blame for marital break-ups. However, conducting weddings means you are already involved in the messiness of life. So, I would conduct the wedding of a divorcee where their previous spouse had committed adultery, where they had been divorced against their wishes, or where their previous spouse had already remarried. The crucial factor in each of these cases is that the previous marriage has genuinely ended, and that the new marriage cannot therefore be adultery. In some situations, I might speak to their former spouse, to hear their side of the story, and explore gently what steps the person had taken since the break-up of their first marriage to seek reconciliation, and how they had learned and grown from the experience.[24] Phrases that ring alarm bells are, 'The marriage didn't work' or 'We drifted apart'. This suggests that there is some third quantity in between the two partners that is at fault, whereas according to the Bible a marriage cannot end itself, but only through the actions of one of the parties. Ministers often have to make tricky judgements and will not always get it right.

Conclusion

Jesus calls us to live according to the way God originally made us. Marriage was created by God to be a lifelong

---

[24]Obviously, there would be times when this would not be appropriate – as in the case of abuse.

union between a woman and a man that reflects God's relationship with his people. That's why you cannot leave a marriage in the same way you entered it, namely by making a decision. But marriage *can* be dissolved by the actions of the other person – either adultery/sexual unfaithfulness or by them initiating divorce. So no one should initiate divorce, except for adultery, but neither is anyone obliged to contest a divorce. A victim of divorce or adultery is free to remarry, as is someone whose previous spouse has remarried.

According to Jesus, remarriage after divorce is often adultery because the previous marriage still exists. So, approach remarriage with caution. Only remarry if you are sure that the previous marriage is over (i.e. because your previous spouse committed adultery, because they initiated the divorce or because they have since remarried).

Reconciliation and restoration are wonderful, but not always possible – for example, when an abusive person professes repentance but is unwilling to make amends and seek proper help. Although I do not think domestic abuse of itself makes it right to initiate a divorce, a person experiencing abuse is not obliged to stay with their spouse. I know this is asking something incredibly difficult, but it does seem to me that adultery is the only time that Jesus allowed someone to initiate divorce.

Marriage isn't easy (but then neither is singleness). But it is a beautiful gift that God has given to humanity to show us something of who God is. For those who are married, it also has the potential to be a place in which another person confronts and knows us at our deepest level, yet loves and accepts us for who we are. That is profoundly life-changing and transforming. Yet precisely because of its depth, marriage is deeply risky and therefore devastating when it falls apart. I hope I have challenged you to stick with and/or support marriage, but also encouraged you with a fresh sense of the security that God bestows on it. After all, it is God who joins people together. So, ultimately and thankfully, the success of marriage does not depend on us.

Go Deeper

Andrew Cornes, *Divorce and Remarriage: Biblical Principles and Pastoral Practice* (Tain: Christian Focus, 2002).

David Instone-Brewer, *Divorce and Remarriage in the Church: Biblical Solutions for Pastoral Realities* (Milton Keynes: Paternoster, 2011).

Barbara Roberts, *Not Under Bondage: Biblical Divorce for Abuse, Adultery and Desertion* (Australia: Maschil Press, 2008).

Mark L. Strauss (ed.), *Remarriage After Divorce in Today's Church: Three Views* (Grand Rapids, MI: Zondervan, 2006).